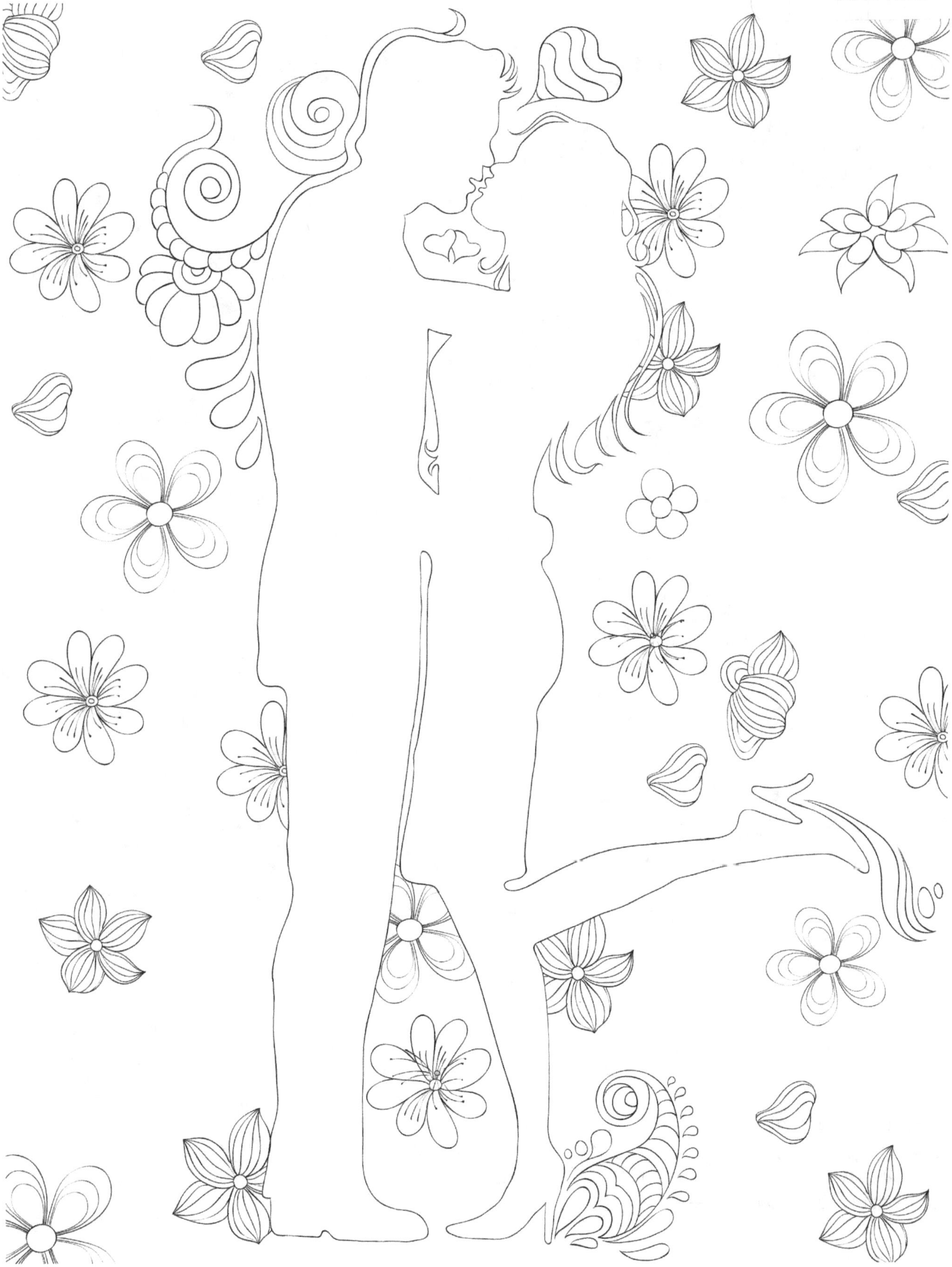

ISBN: 978-1523369317
by: Adult Coloring Book Sets
(Illustrated by: Mandala & Caricature Illustration)

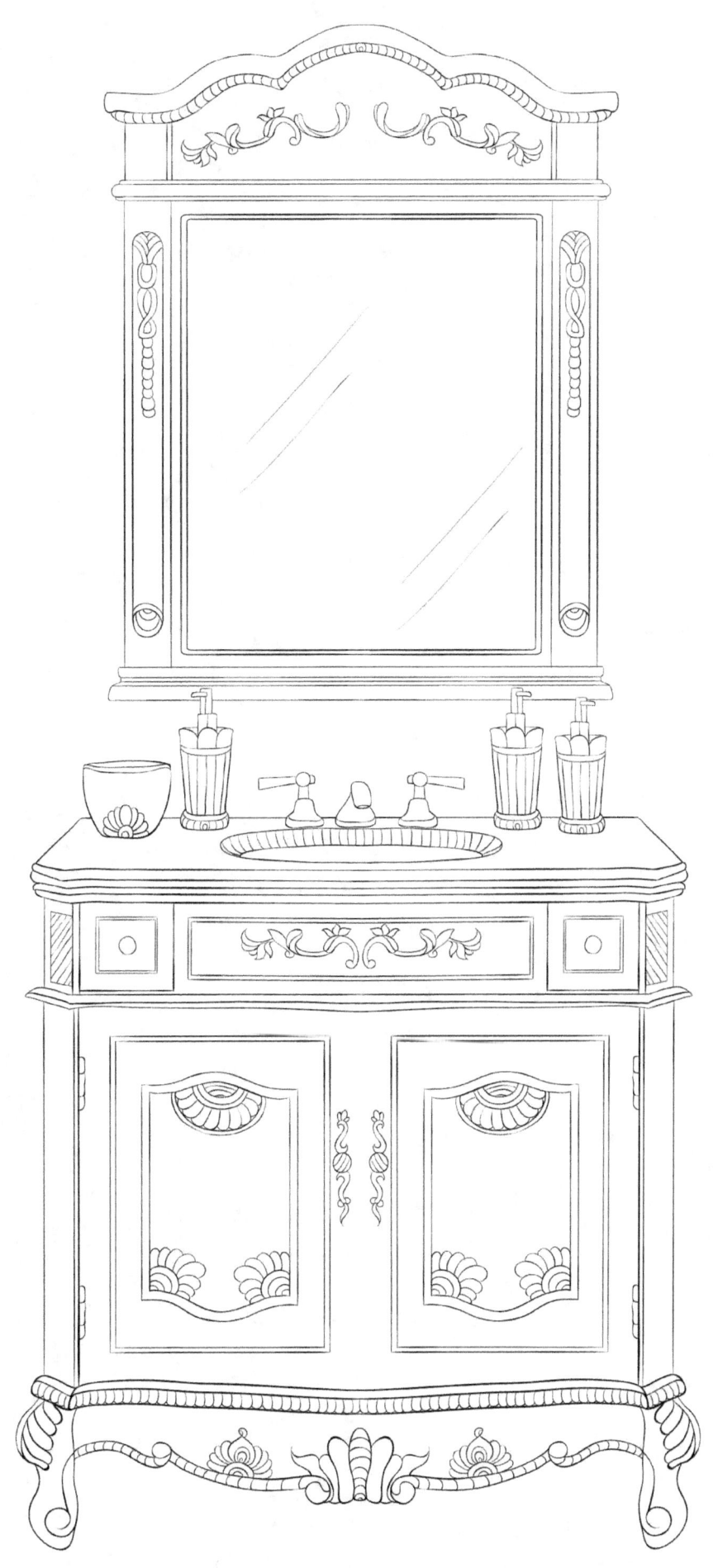

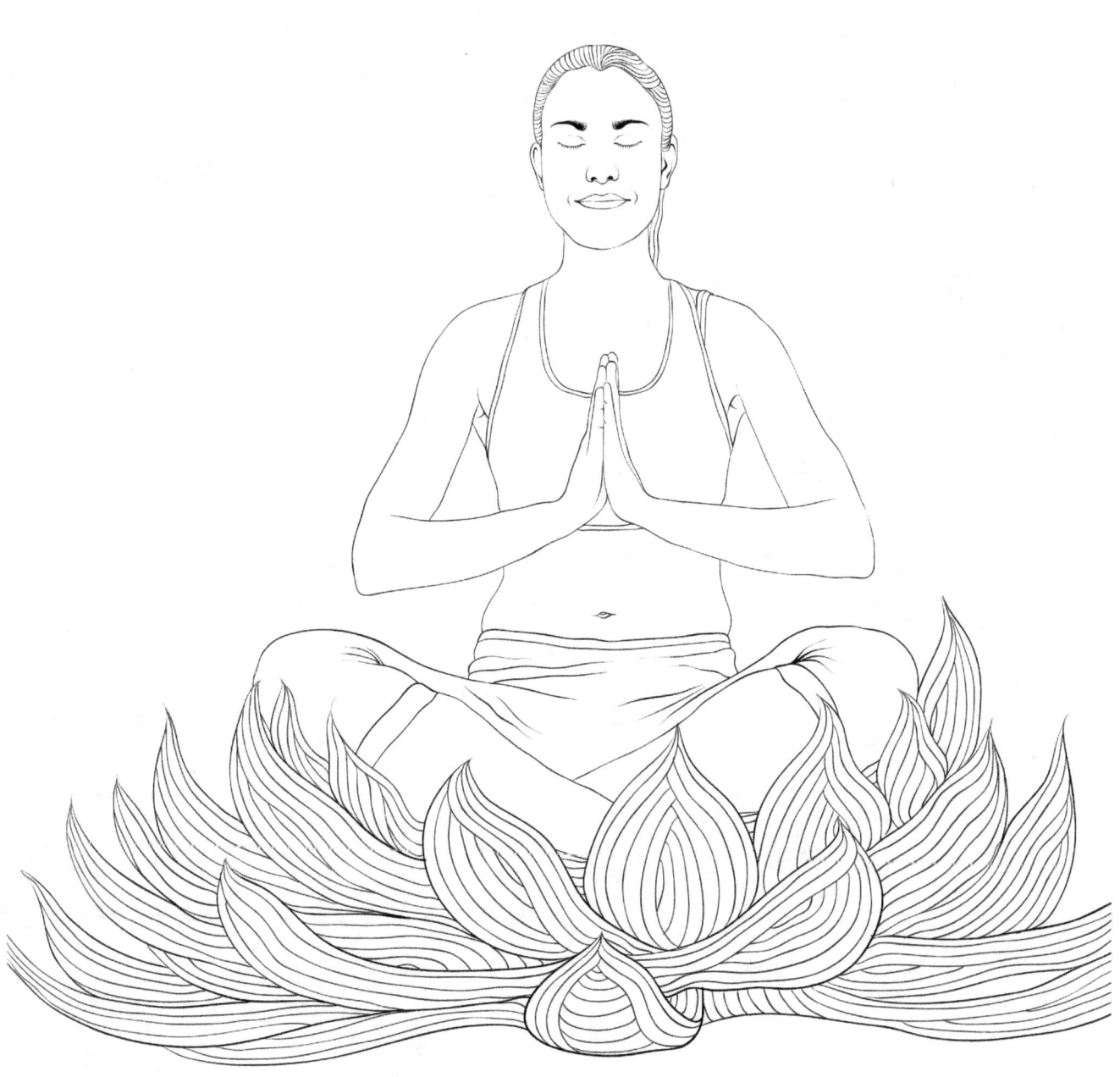

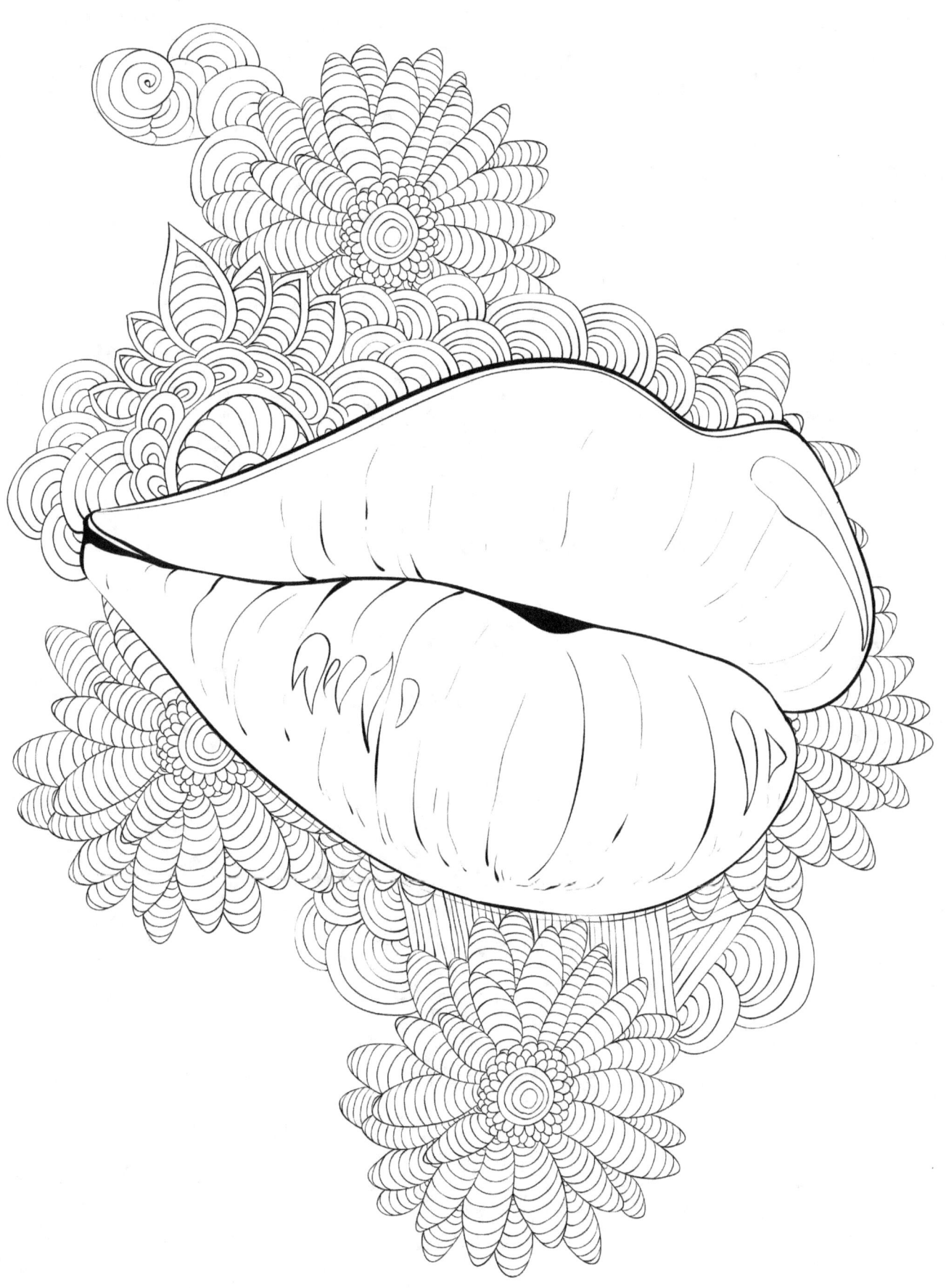

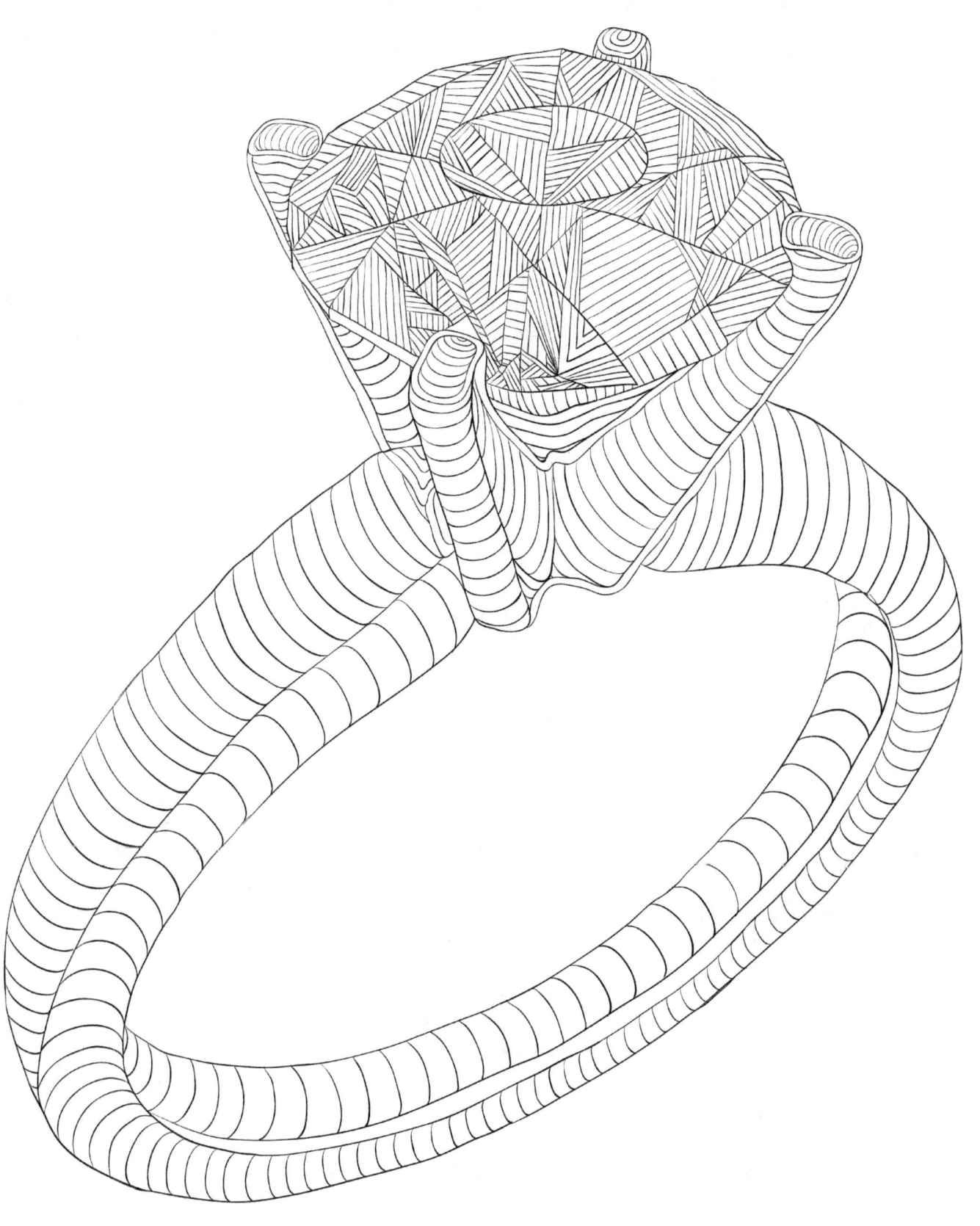

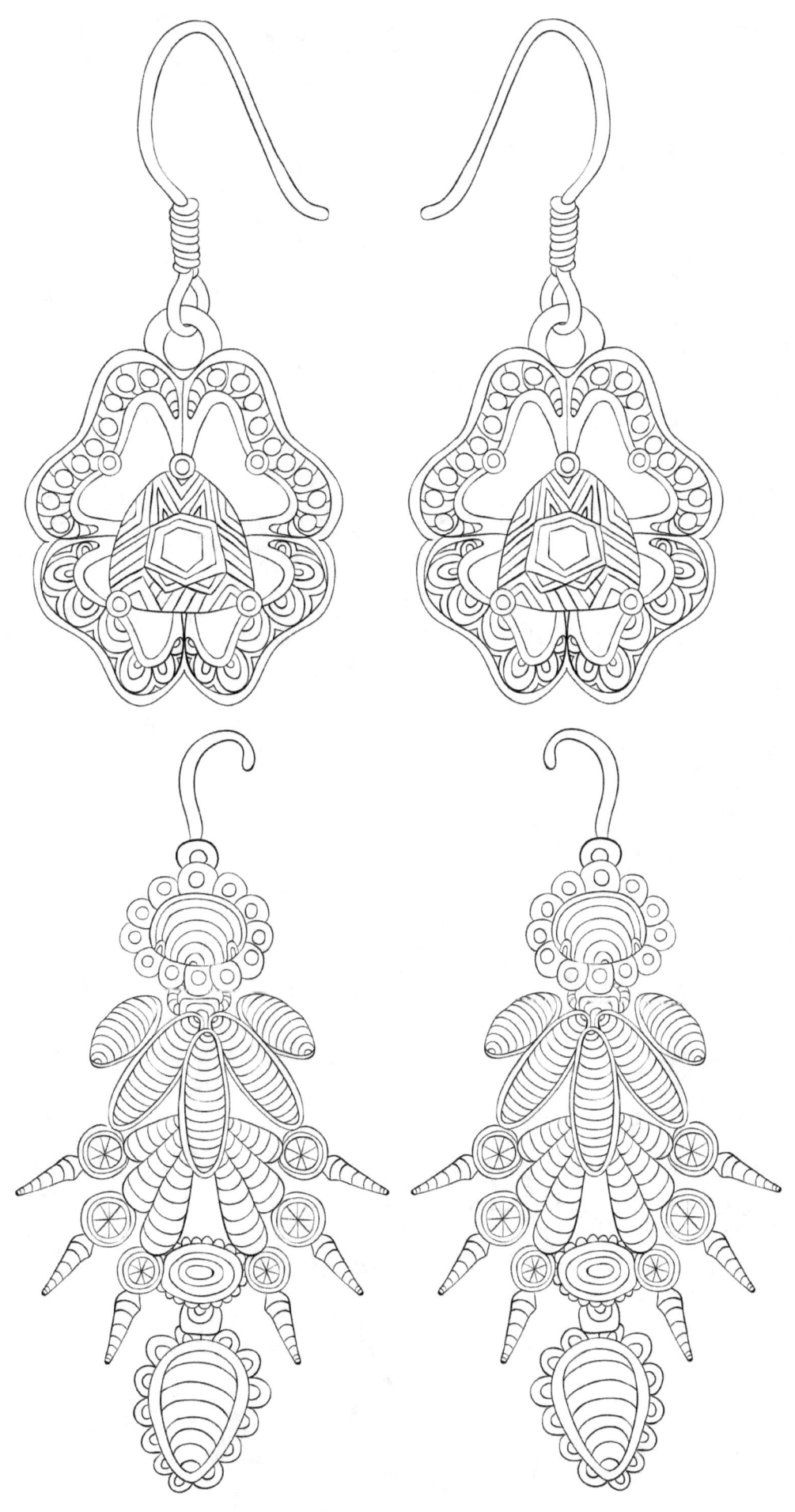

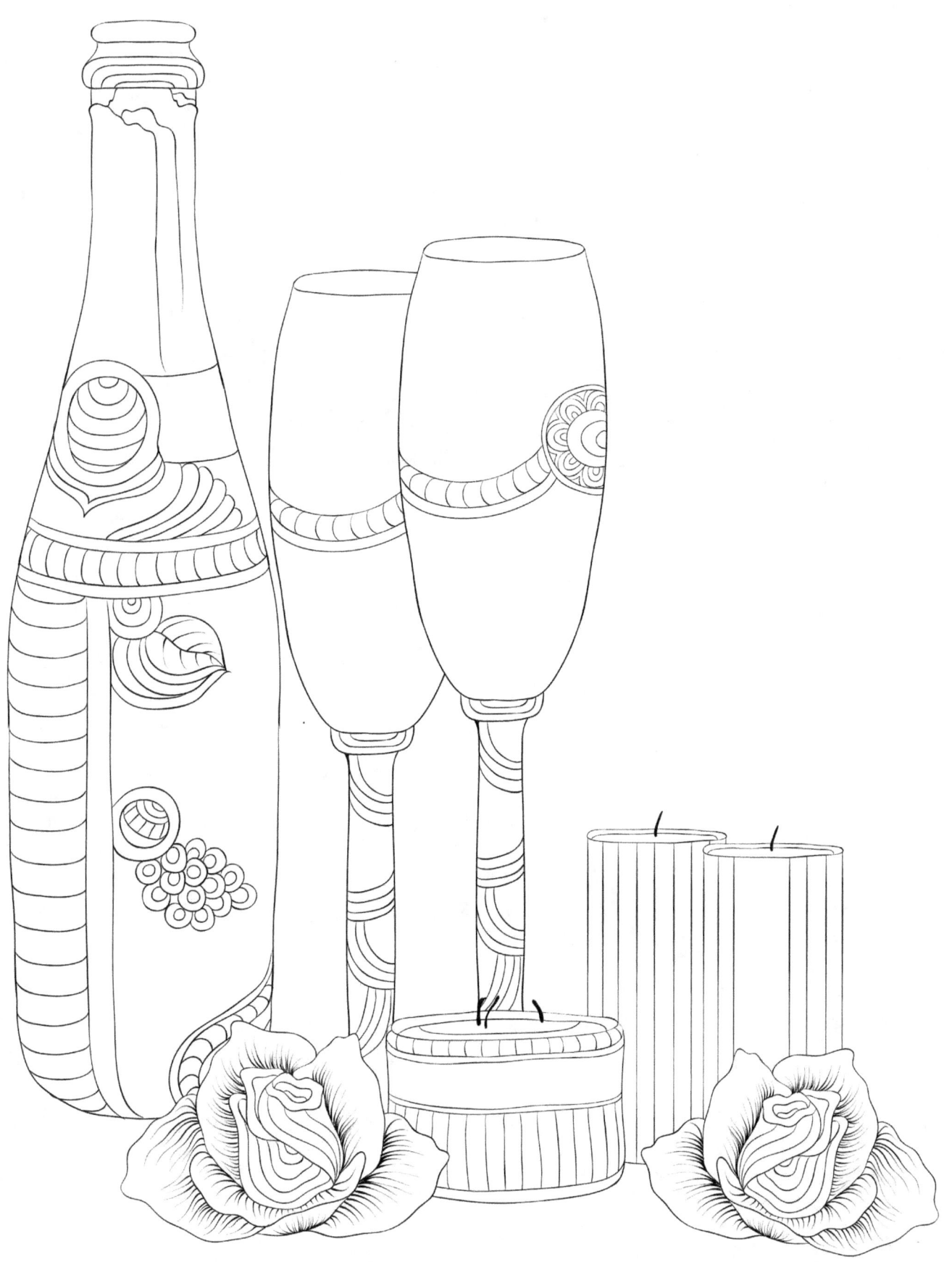

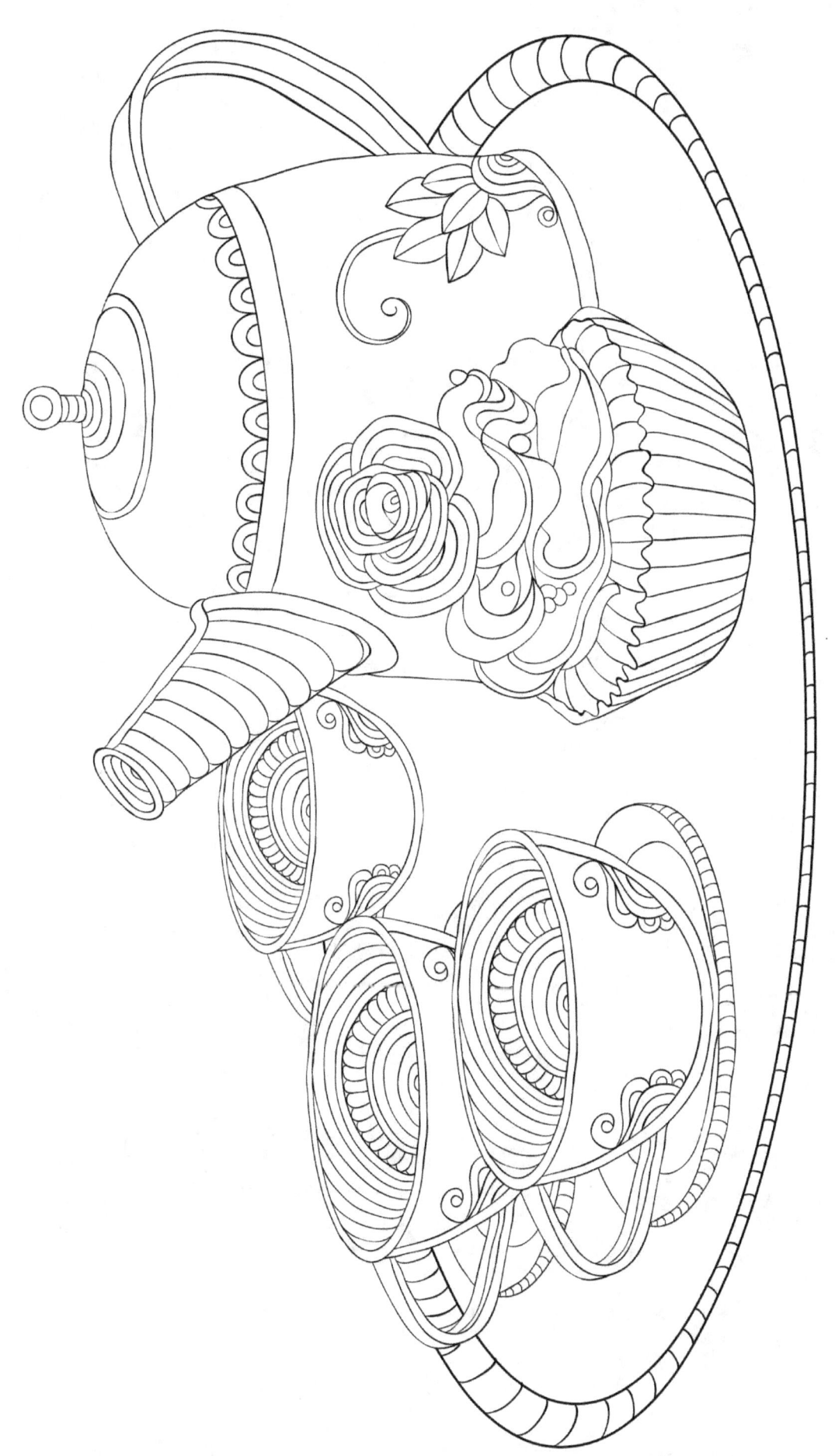

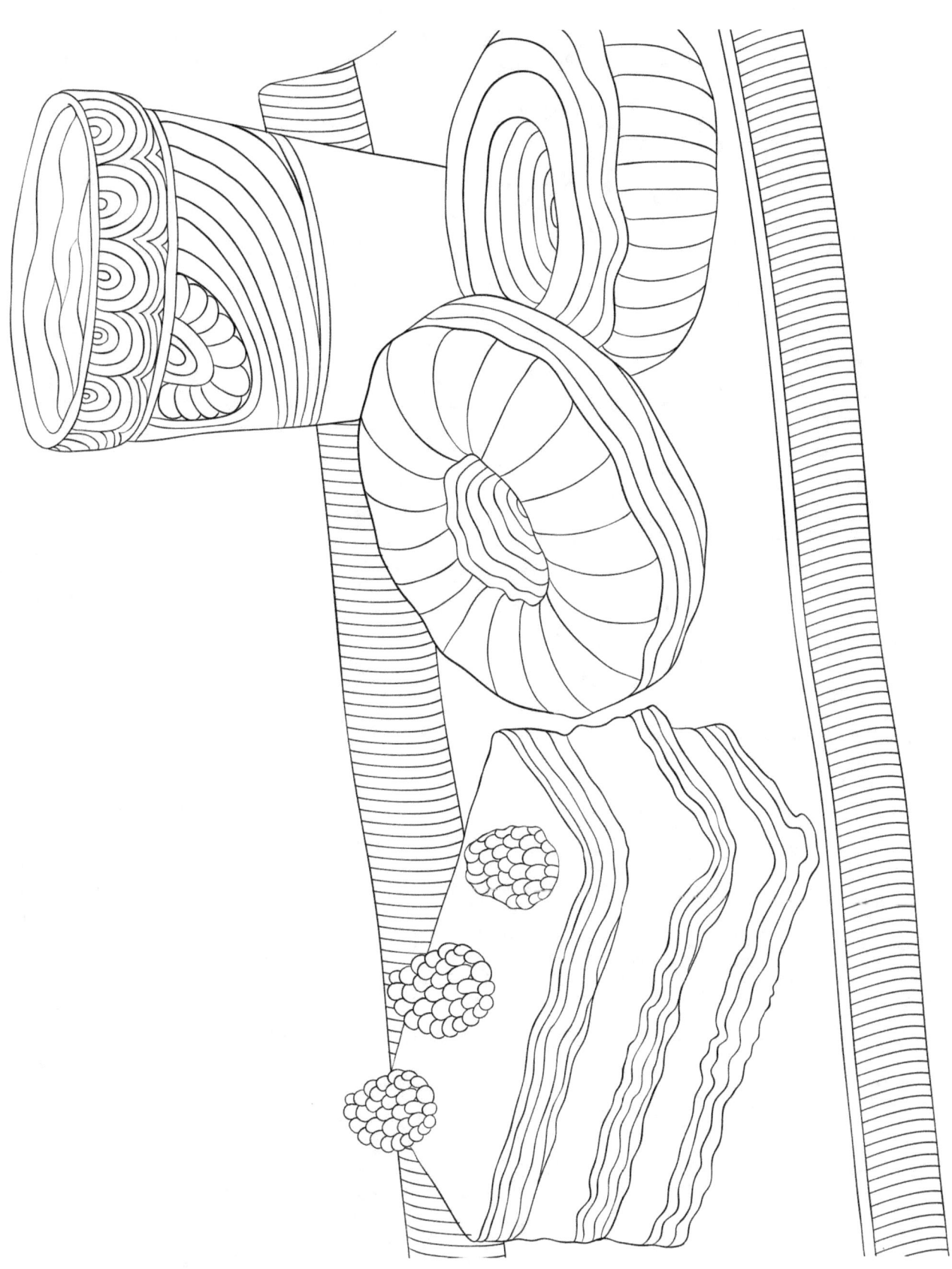

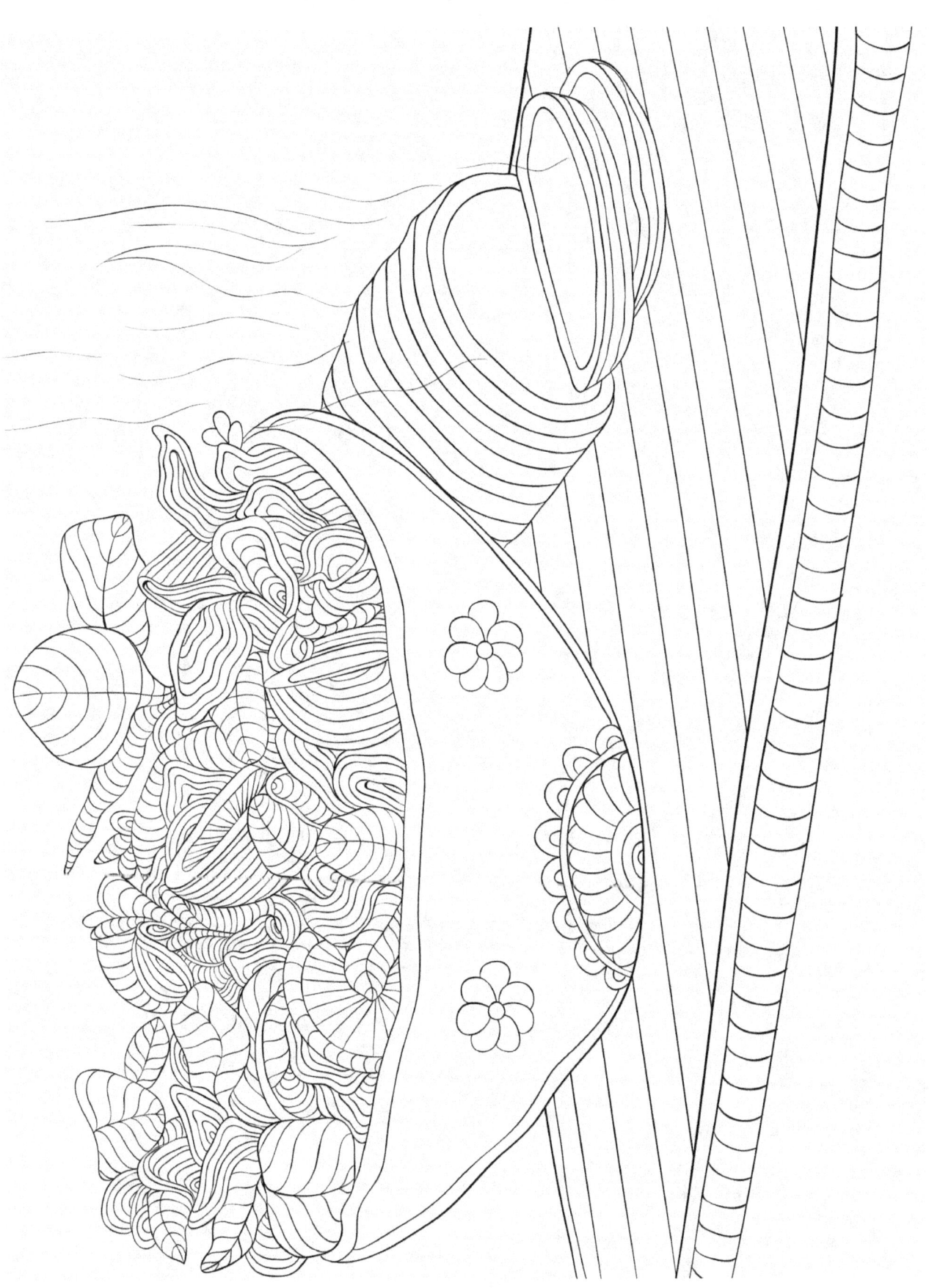

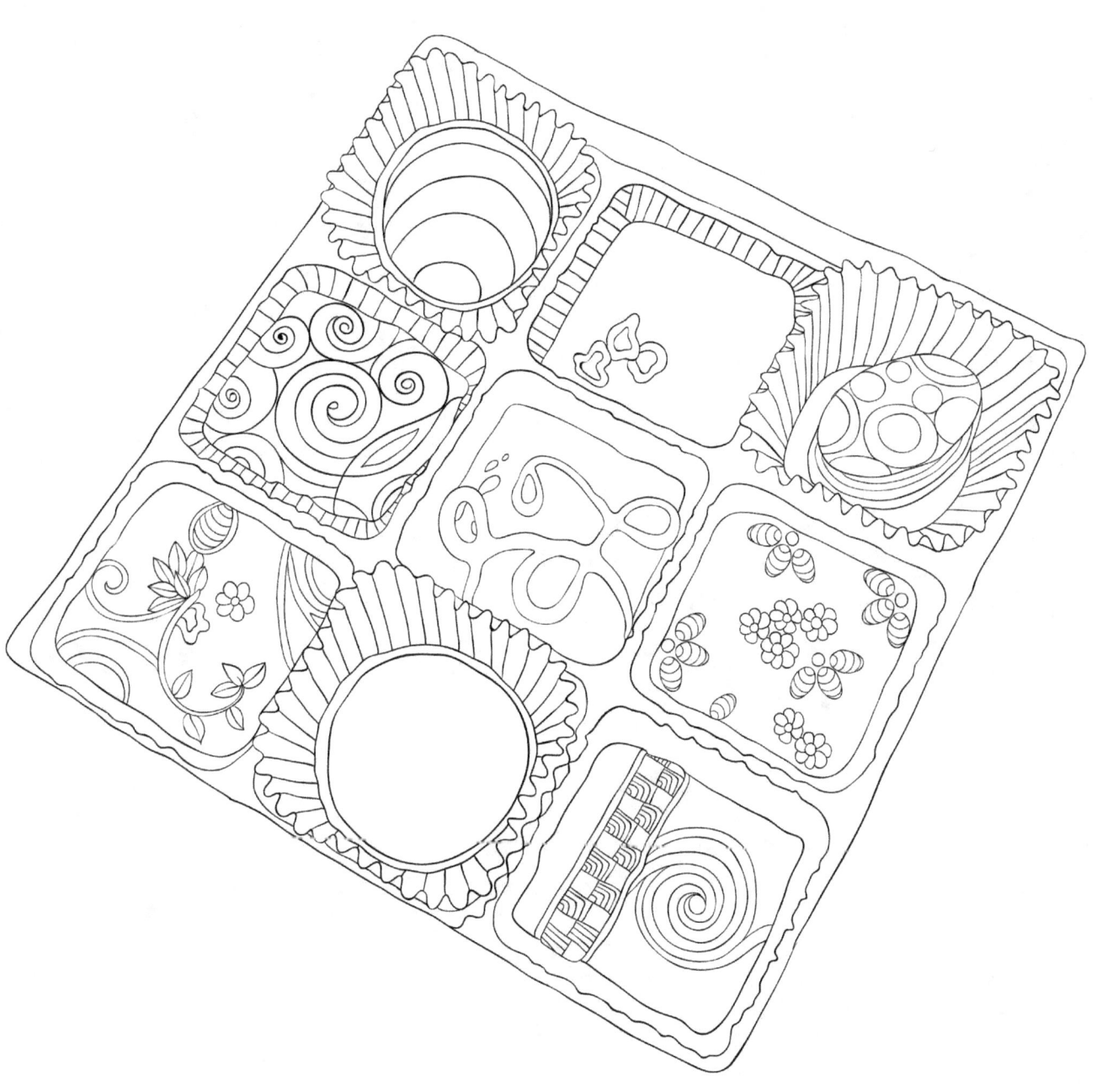

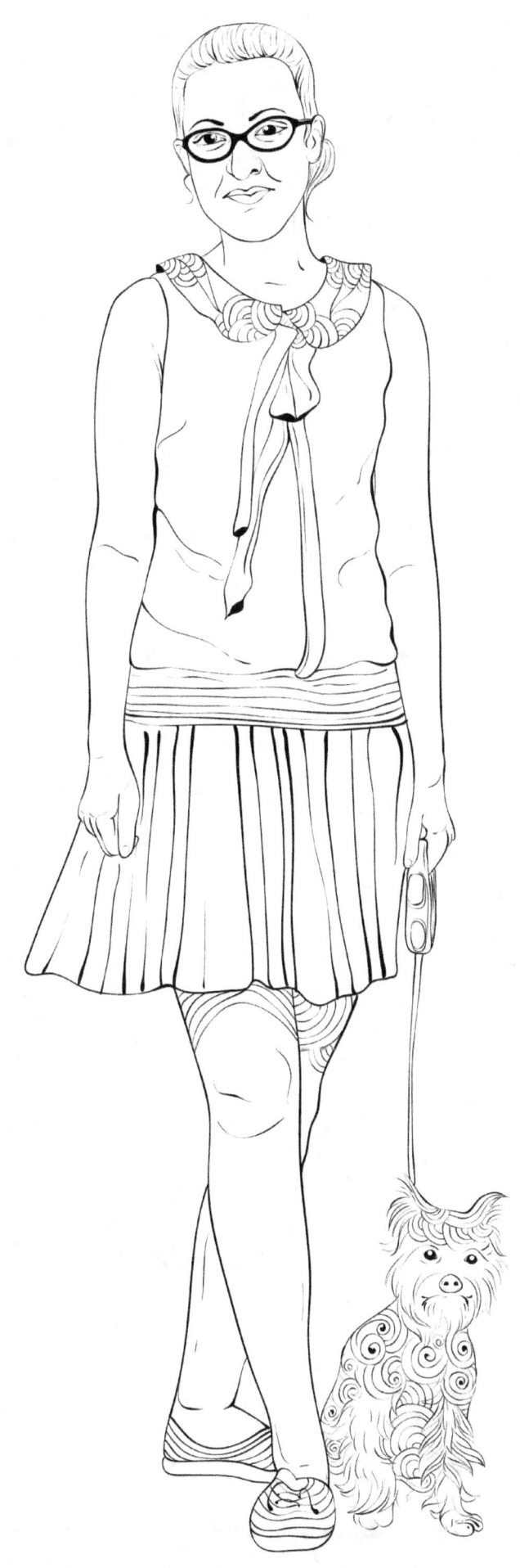

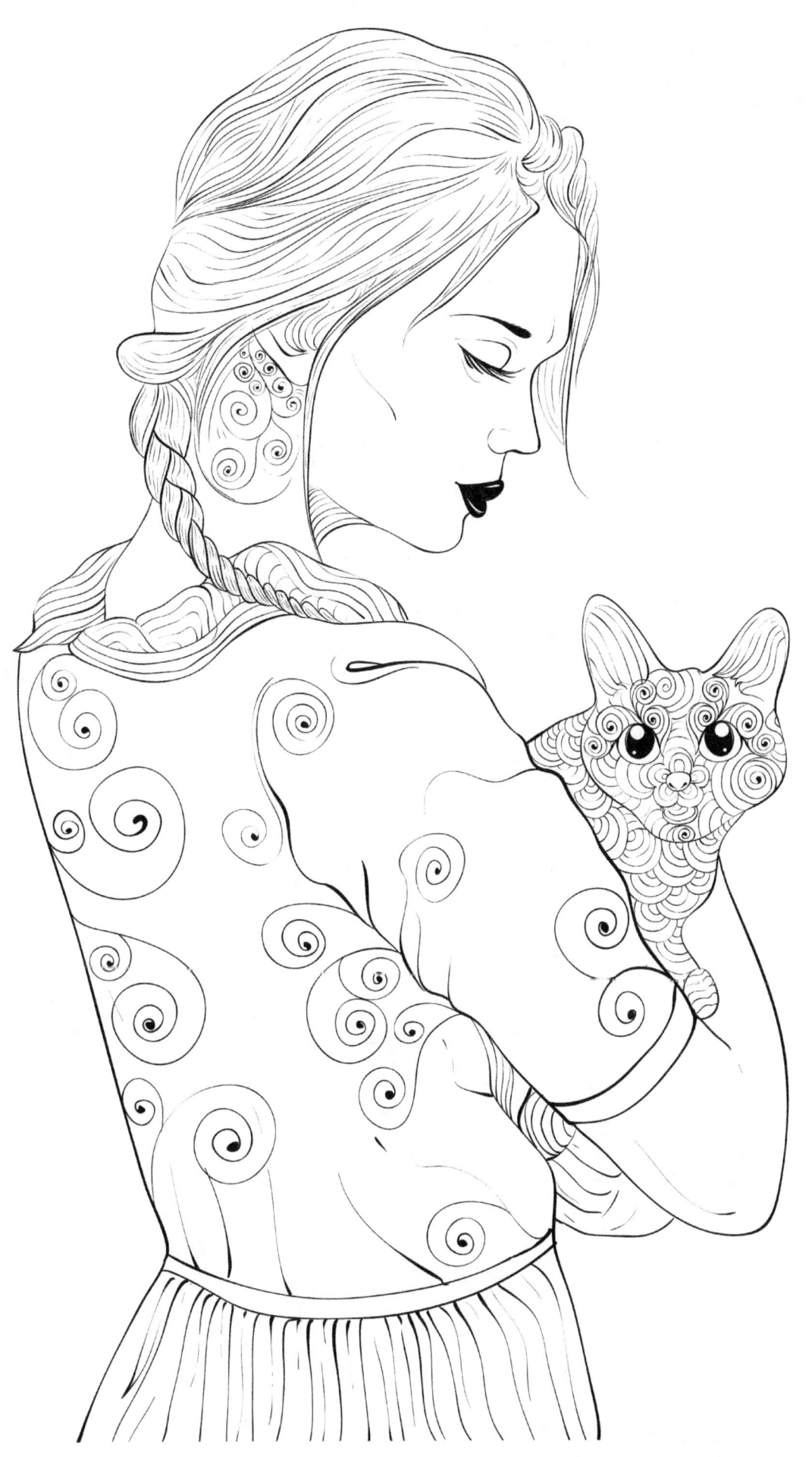

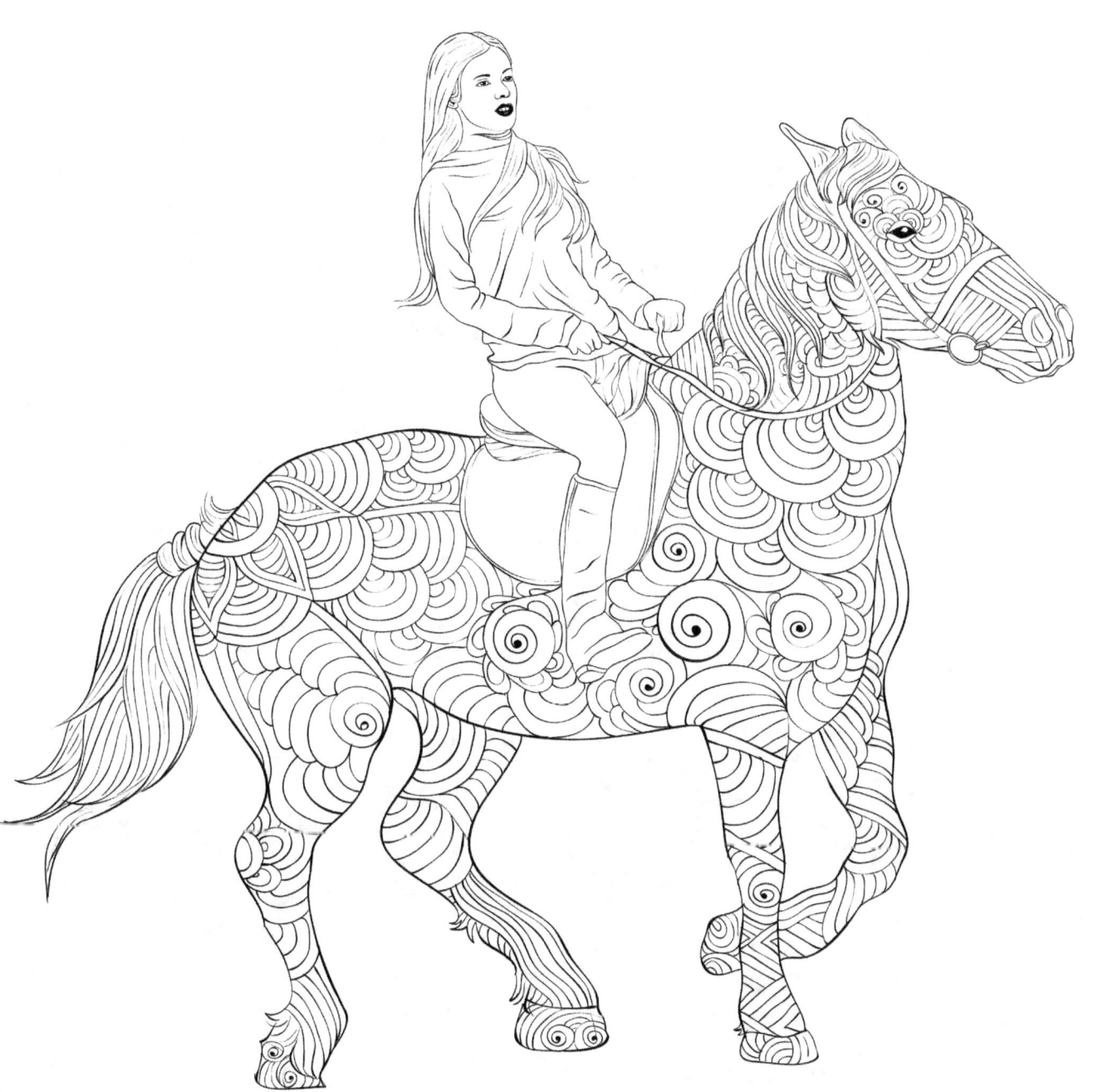

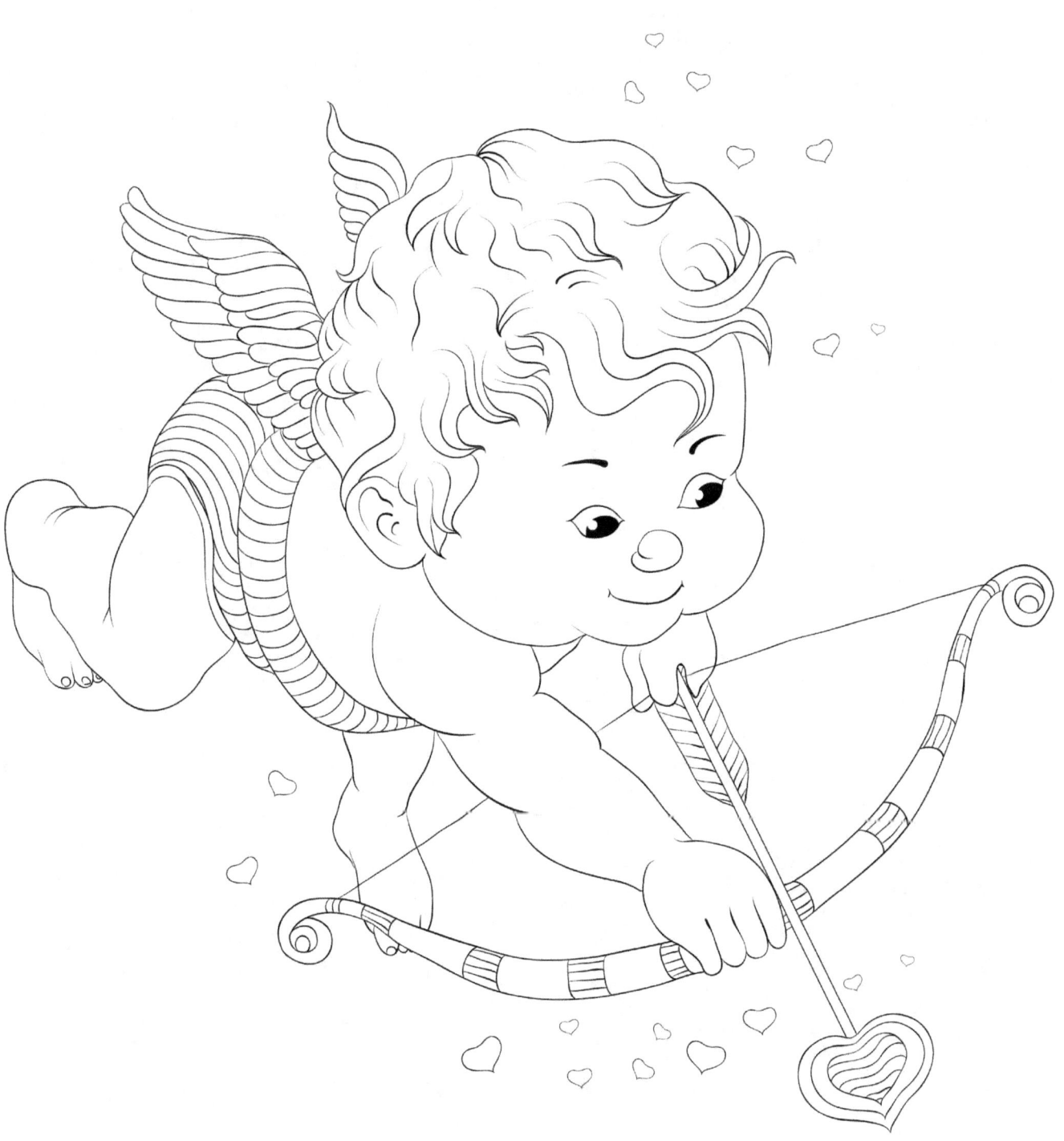

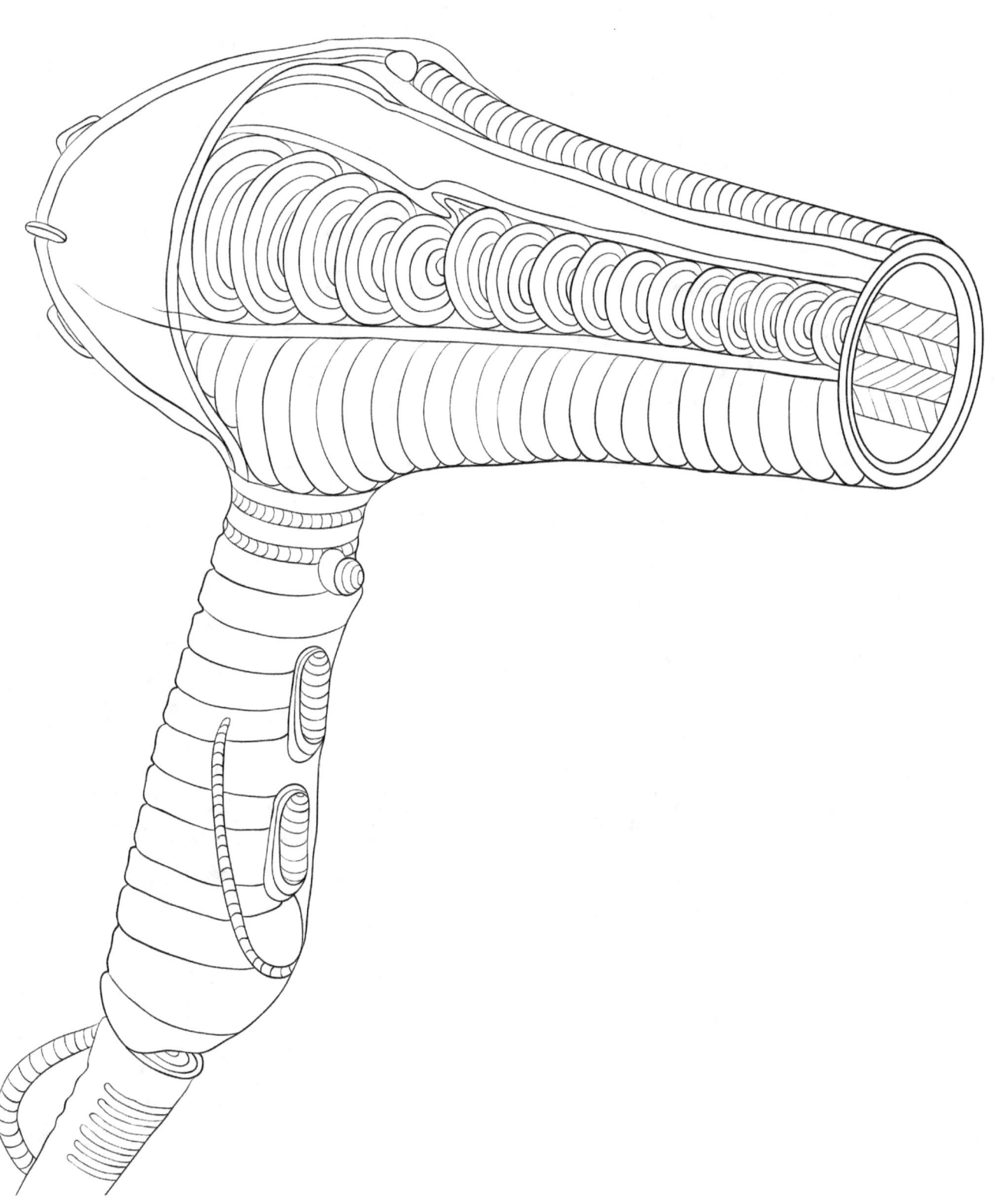

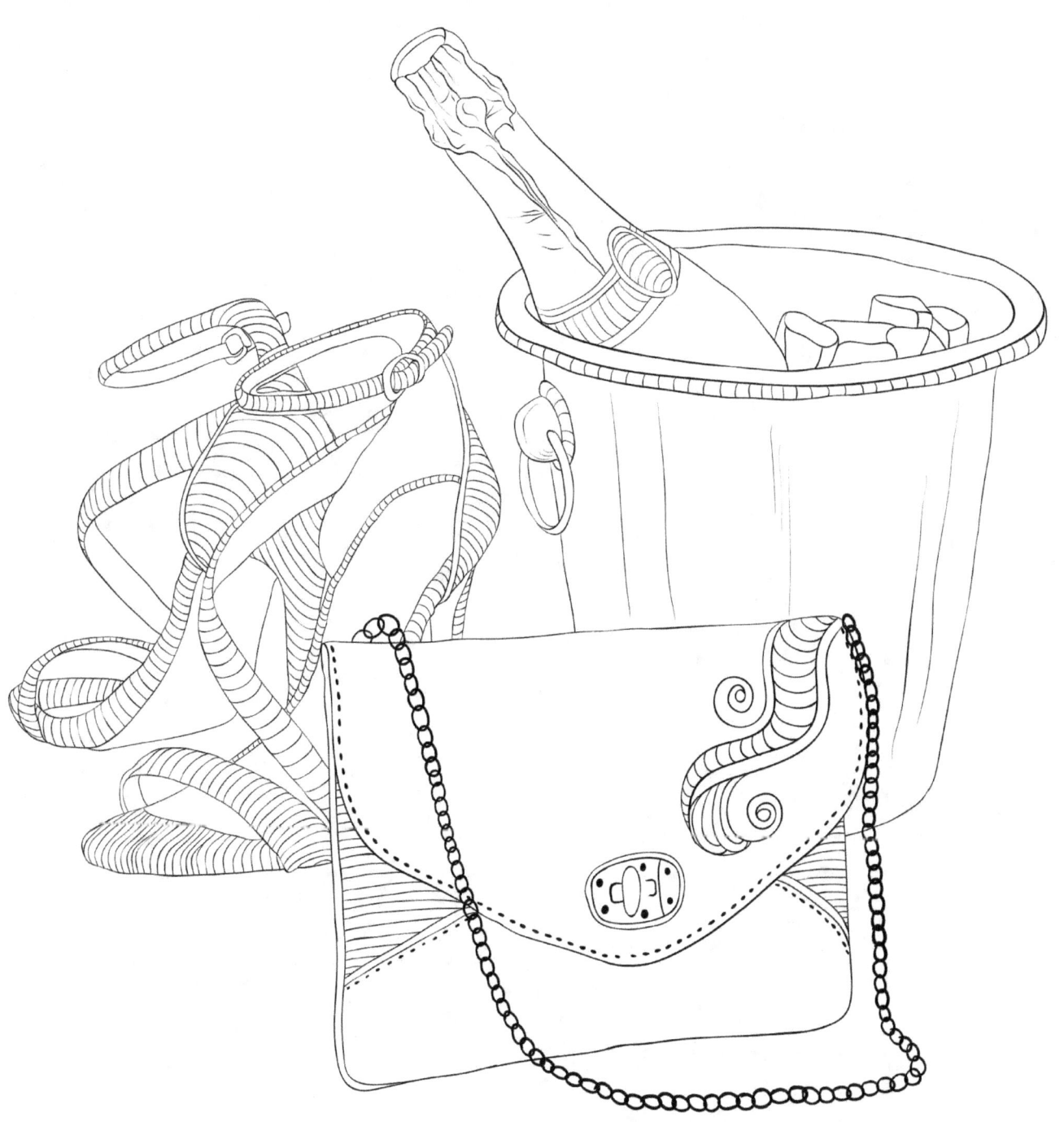

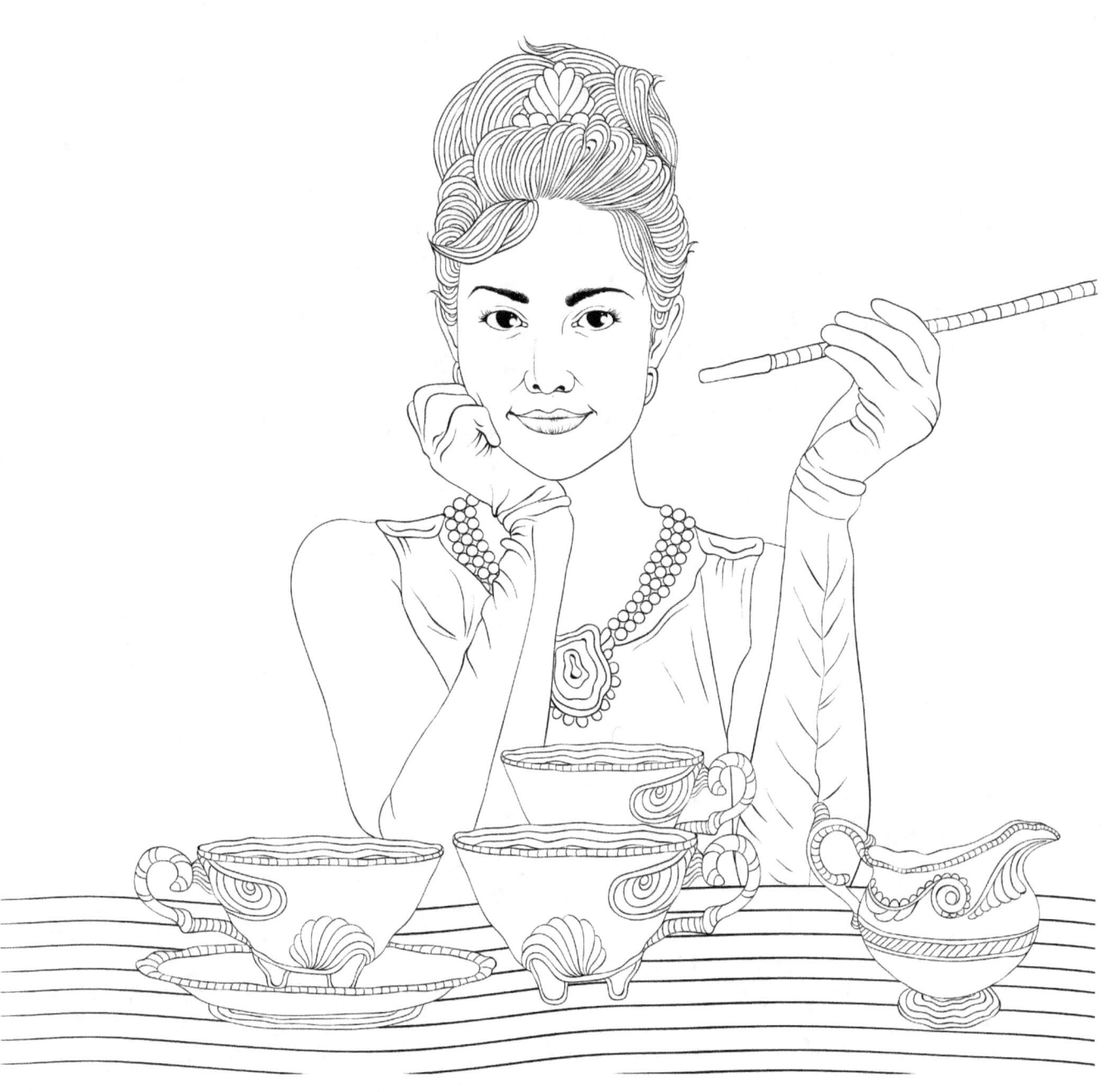

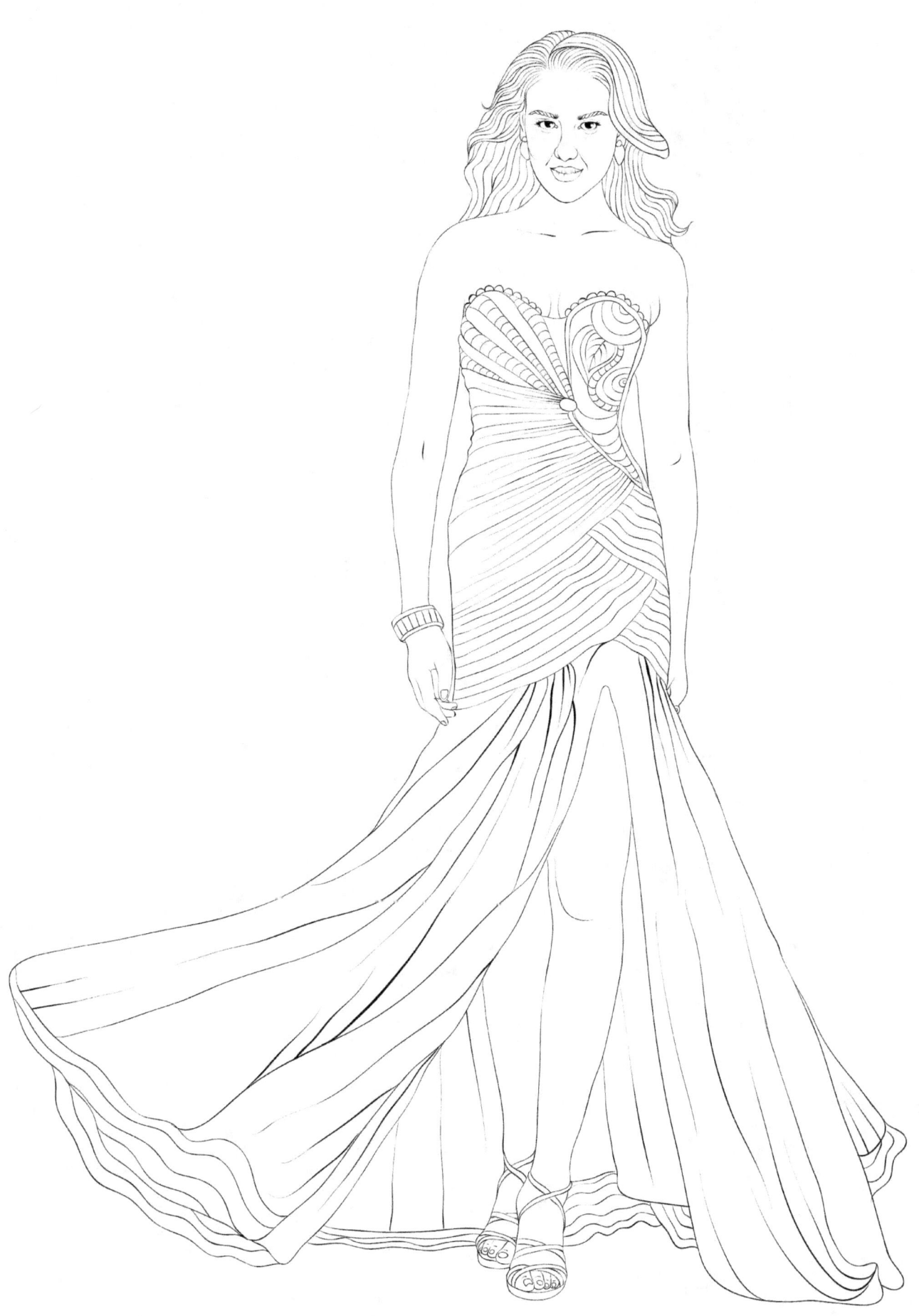

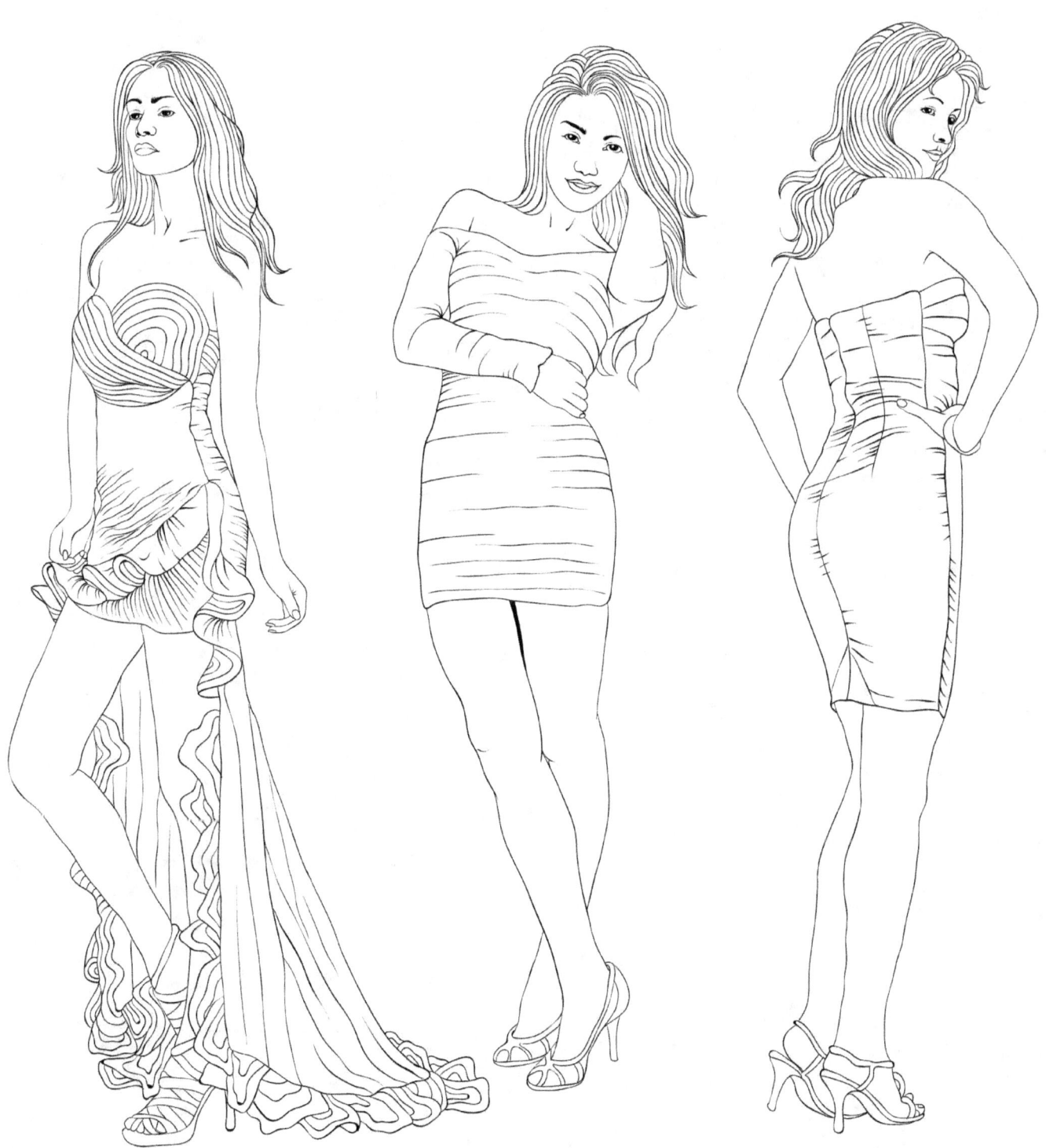

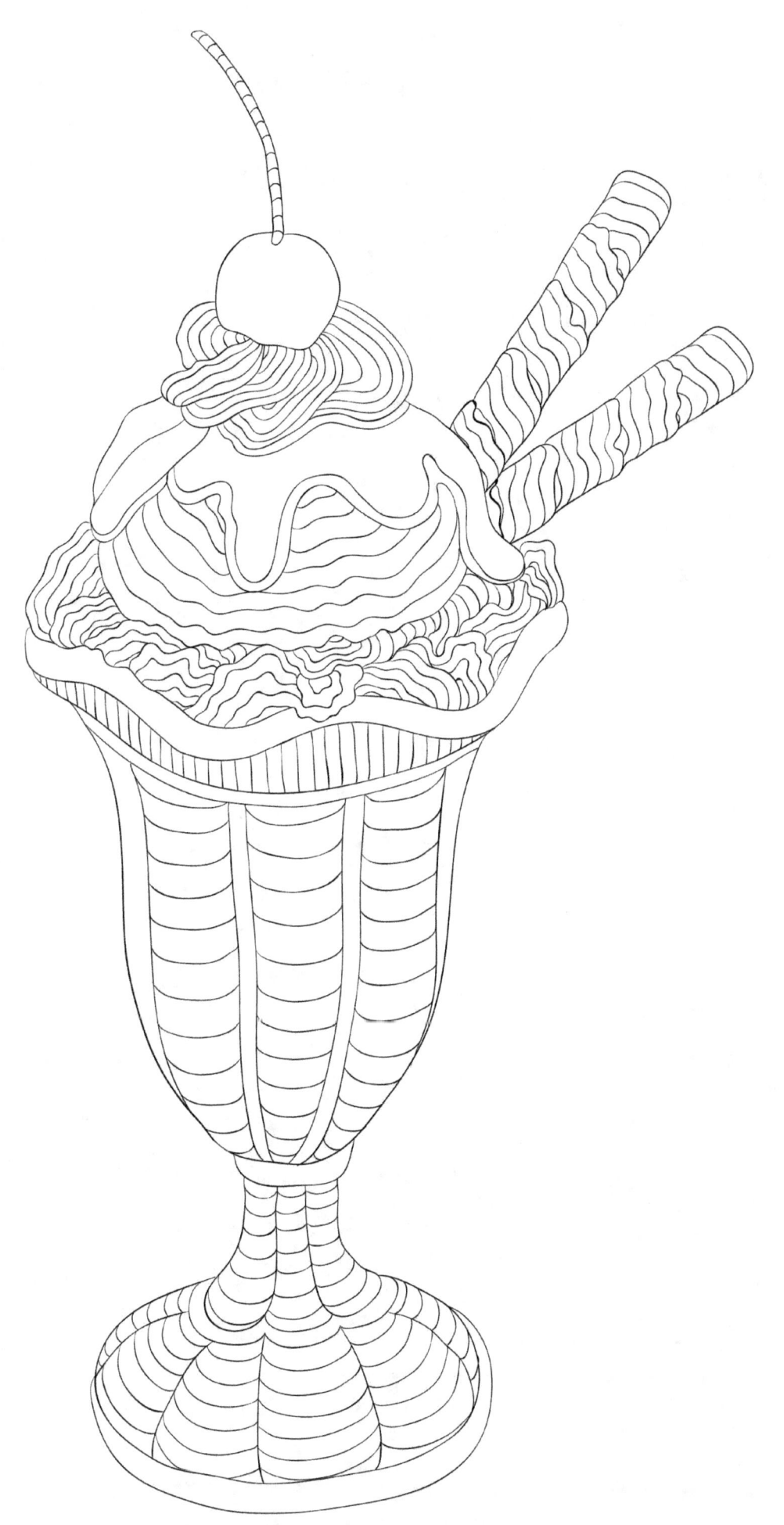

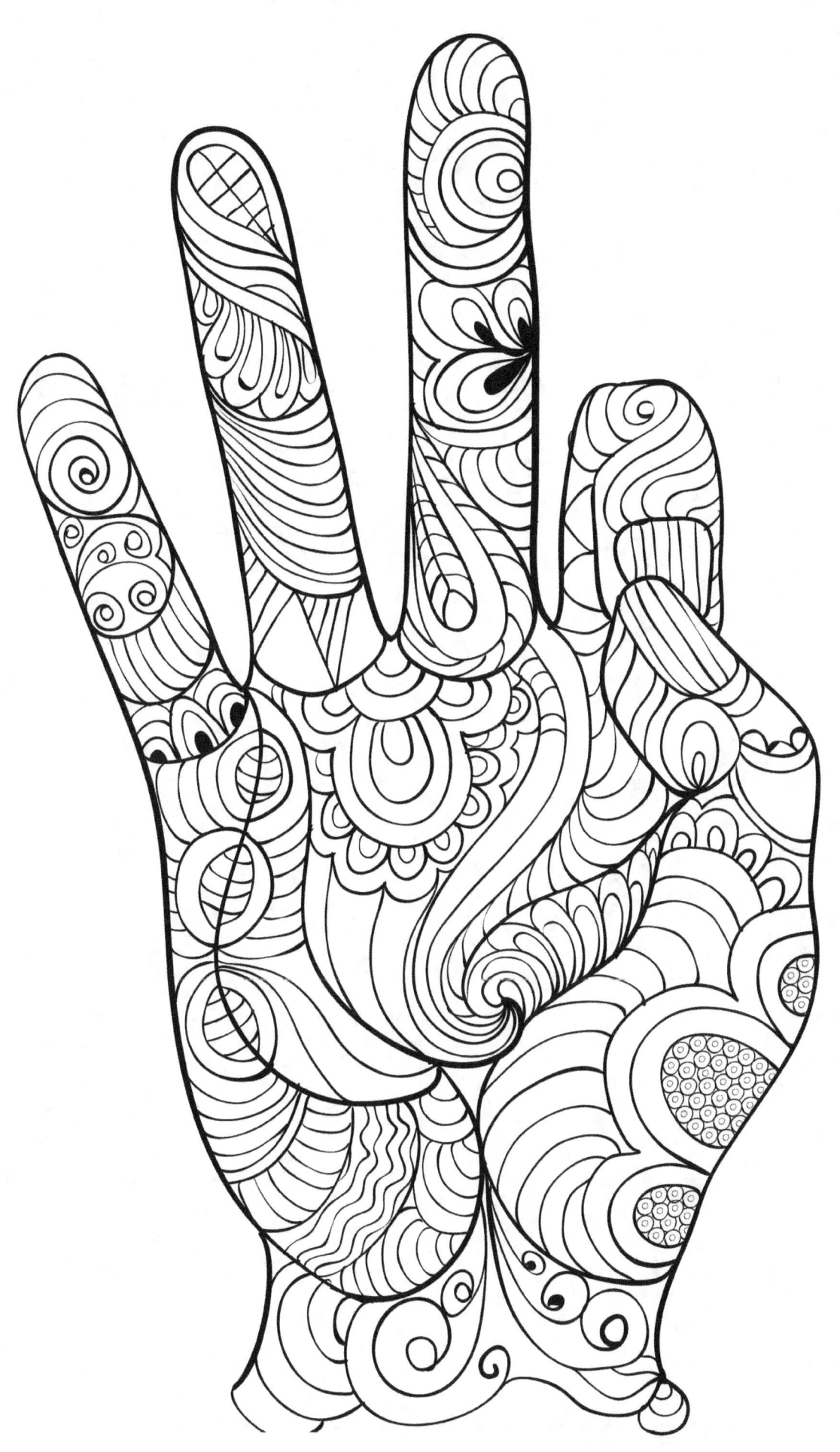

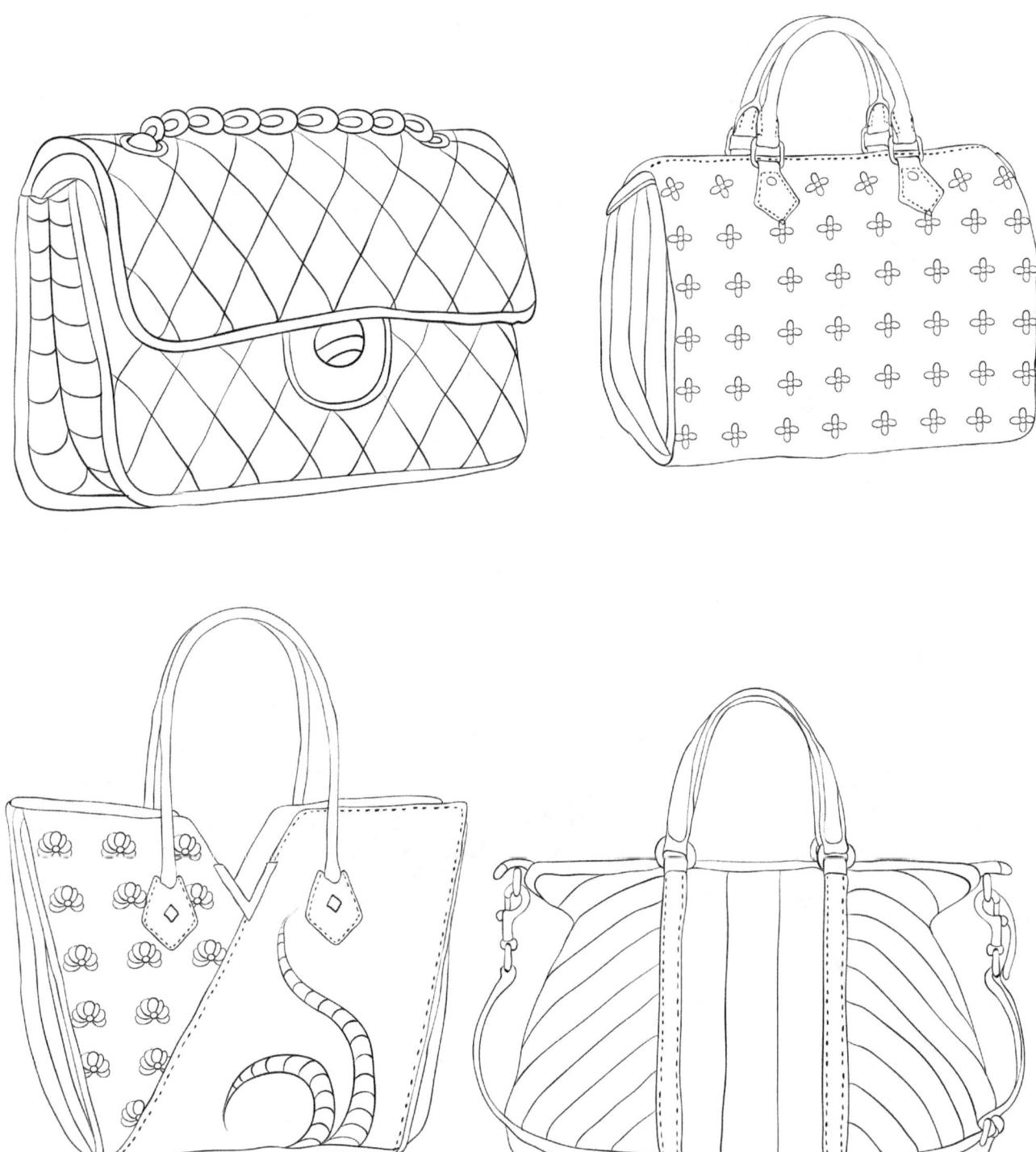

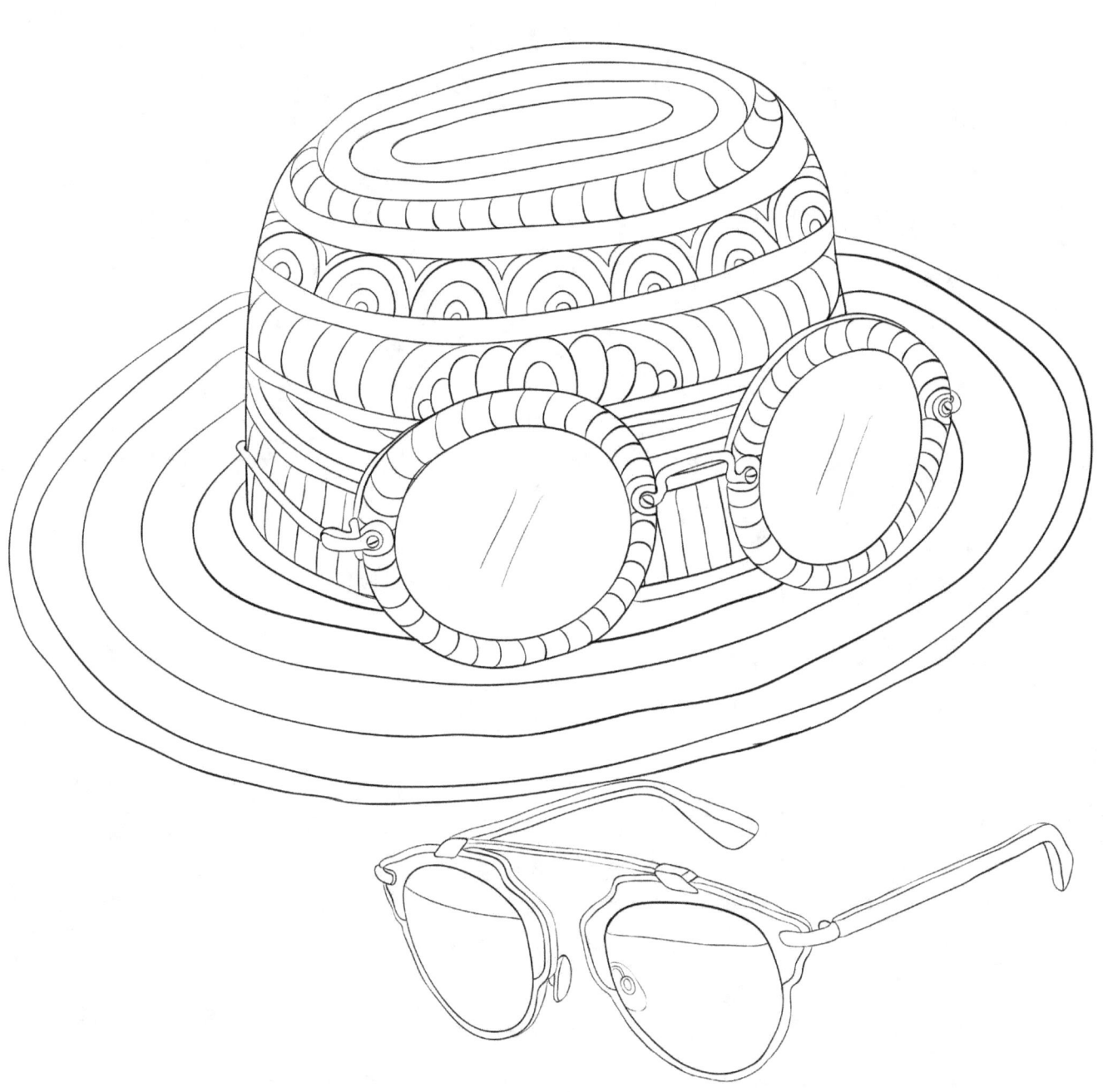

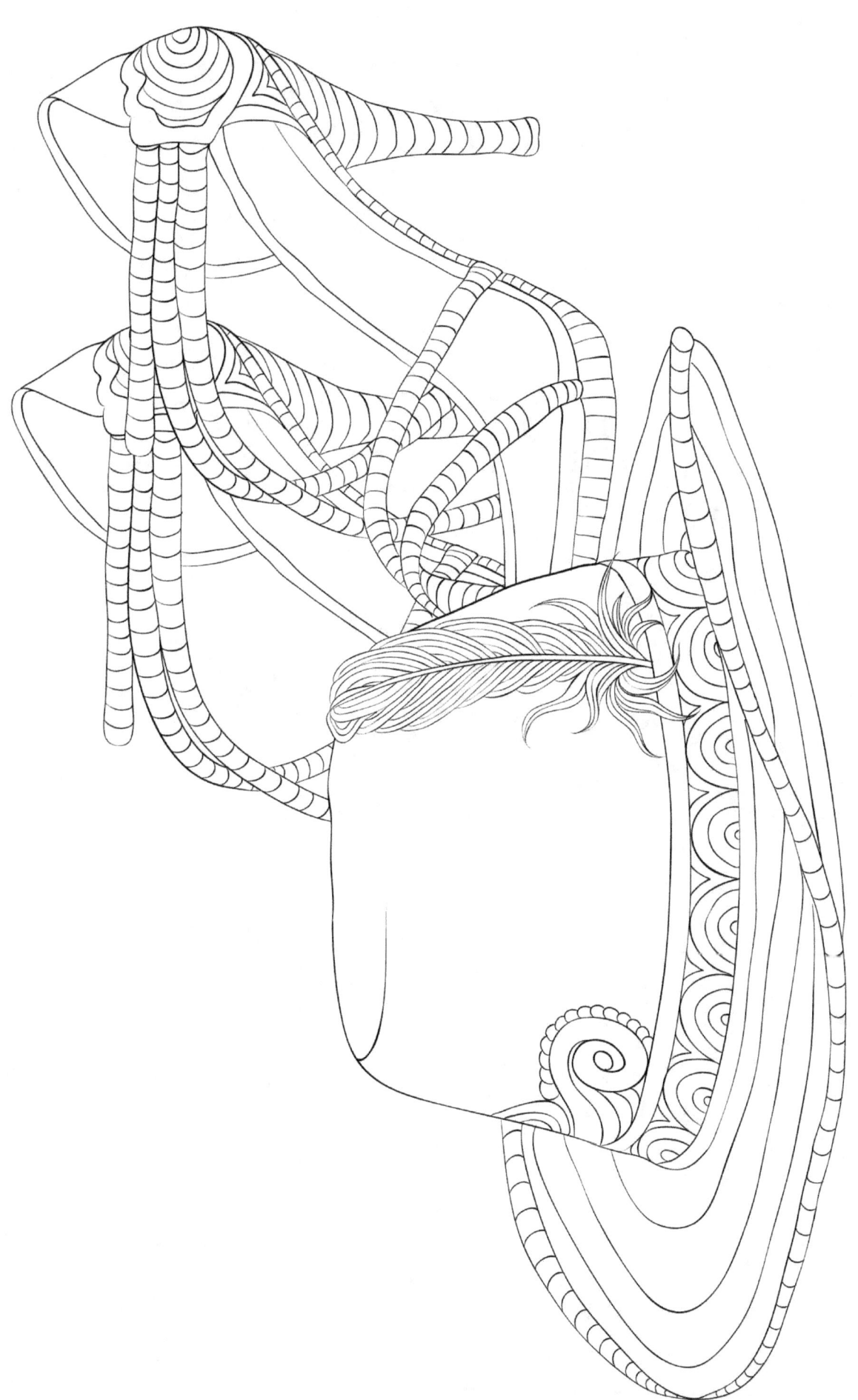

Free Bonus Book

$3.99 value electronic coloring book, easy to print out. Download your FREE book now:

http://CoolAdultColoringBooks.com

More: Check our website above for new books and special promotion deals…